Snowflake Buddies: ABC Leftism for Kids!

by Lewis Liberman

The 2nd French Revolution

Snowflake Buddies: ABC Leftism for Kids!
Copyright © 2018 by Lewis Liberman

ALL RIGHTS RESERVED. No part of this publication may be reproduced, distributed, or transmitted in any form or by any means, including photocopying, recording, or other electronic or mechanical methods, or by any information storage and retrieval system without the prior written permission of the publisher, except in the case of very brief quotations embodied in critical reviews and certain other non-commercial uses permitted by copyright law.

Produced in the REPUBLIC OF SOUTH CAROLINA by

SHOTWELL PUBLISHING, LLC
Post Office Box 2592
Columbia, South Carolina 29202

www.ShotwellPublishing.com

Cover Design: Lewis Liberman

ISBN-13: 978-1-947660-99-1
ISBN-10: 1-947660-99-3

10 9 8 7 6 5 4 3 2 1

Thank You!

Thank you for reading our little book, and learning more about how Leftism is shaping our world today! Created with current public school standards in mind, our book is ideal for teaching the alphabet while also reinforcing all that the Left holds dear. We are also proud to bear the seal of the Society of the Golden Pacifier, which recognized our ABC's of Leftism as "one of the most important works for Leftists!" Enjoy!

A is for Antifa Al!

Antifa Al stomped and hissed,
and called your mom a big Fascist.
And when you shared a different case?
He smashed his bat right into your face.

B is for Barbara Belle!

Barbara Belle is a leftist too,
and went to a rally to yell at you.
But when you differed over what she said,
She dumped some pee all over your head.

C is for Commie Carl!

Commie Carl works on taxpayer dime,
crafting laws that punish made-up crimes.
Through a standing army he determines your fate.
With tanks and guns, it's a Police State.

D is for Doctor Doug!

Doctor Doug, in the university he works.
Tearing down Christianity is where he lurks.
On the virtues of leftism he often teaches.
He has no God, but on Statism he preaches.

E is for Earl the Economist!

Earl the Economist is a proud Keynesian man.
Dollars spring forth when poop hits the fan.
Rothbard or Mises, he will never preserve.
Cause this man defends the federal reserve.

F is for Fran the Feminist!

Fran the Feminist wants you to run and hide,
and shut up about the abortion genocide.
Your right to free speech she doesn't give a rip.
You like that too? It's called censorship.

G is for Greg the Globalist!

Greg the Globalist is a one world man,
but of logistics and reality, he's not a fan.
On his sci-fi utopia he raves and spews,
all while hating you for your secessionist views.

H is for Huey the Homosexual!

Huey the Homosexual wants to force his way,
and demands you celebrate him, just because he is gay.
Of course he is free to love, this is nothing new.
But now he wants the State to force it on you.

I is for Ira the Instigator!

Ira the Instigator loves a good fight,
especially when it has to do with the Right.
But being selective is how he wins his game,
as he only fights that which yields fortune and fame.

J is for Judge Jasmine!

Jasmine the Judge sees herself as a black robed god.

Upon the Constitution and Bible she doth proudly trod.

Precedent and loopholes are what she will use,

to make sure her enemies are the ones who will lose.

K is for Kara the Kindergarten Teacher!

Kara the Kindergarten Teacher molds young minds,

with Marxist ideology, she happily blinds.

The public school system she devoutly defends,

and unknowingly to Hell, a generation she sends.

L is for Lester the Lincoln Lover!

Lester the Lincoln lover, about his hero he raves.

He thinks the "Civil War" was about freeing the slaves.

He worships at Abe's temple in Washington D.C.,

and smashes Southern monuments

with absolute glee.

M is for Mia the Marxist!

Mia the Marxist wears a Che Guevera shirt,

and if you're a Southerner, she'll treat you like dirt.

She'll dox and ruin you through her commie blog,

and recommend you be sent to a State run gulag.

N is for Nancy the News Anchor!

Nancy the News Anchor is a show business star,

with wit, charm and bias, she's a propaganda star.

She follows the script, and is a household name,

and as long as she's useful, she will know no shame.

O is for Oliver the Offended!

Oliver the Offended has a big "chip" on his shoulder.

But since he's always so mad, it's now the size of a boulder.

He has a keen eye for stuff that really turns his crank,

so as to slap with a lawsuit, for more dough in the bank.

P is for Pam the Preacher!

Pam the Preacher, of the Church of Good Cheer,
on Biblical truth, she remains quite unclear.
For her, God's Power isn't really as great
as lots of money in an offering plate.

Q is for Quaid the Quack!

Quaid the Quack is a biased, science twit,
but he's on TV, so that means he's legit.
On global warming and sex he studies,
which gains him a lot of leftist buddies.

R is for Rudy the Racist!

Rudy the Racist, for equality he fights.
Still, it's shockingly true that he hates all whites.
He burns their stores, and loves to riot.
And on all this the Left is strangely quiet.

S is for Sam the Statist!

Sam the Statist loves the State, and beneath it all he cowers,
believing nothing can be done, without it's awesome powers.
About taxes you may gripe, and other heavy loads...
but Sam will shrug and smugly say, "What about muh roads?"

T is for Tia the Tolerant!

Tia the Tolerant can be sneakily scary,

as she and her cronies oversee your library.

They cry for more tax dollars, those sly little crooks,

for which to buy and promote more LGBT books.

U is for Uma the Undergraduate

Uma the Undergraduate, is a college punk,

she's always skipping classes, and smells like a skunk.

She thinks she's a hotshot protestor, at a fancy school,

but she's really just another deluded leftist fool.

V is for Vic the Vulgar!

Vulgar Vic? You know his type, he's a nasty pain,

with flippant filthy utterings, spewed from a putrid brain.

Whether at the store or on the Net, he loves to be a troll,

and makes you think that this old world, is just a hell-bound hole.

W is for Wanda the Welfare Queen!

Wanda is a Welfare Queen, she doesn't like to work.

And if you say she needs a job, she'll likely go berserk.

She thinks she's owed "free" money - what a nasty lie of heft!

Cause when you think about it, taxation is purely theft.

 **is for Xavier the Xenophobe!**

Xavier the Xenophobe is an ironic kind of dude.

If you disagree with him, well buddy then you're screwed.

He claims to value tolerance, but sadly it's not true.

As he really can't stand anyone who doesn't share his view.

Y is for Yoric the Yankee!

Yankee Yoric is not content and likely is quite sick,

as into the lives of others, his nose he will gladly stick.

Near or far, it matters not, he will always find a flaw.

And force his views on many, by creating another law.

Z is for Zania the Zombie

Zania Zombie, is dogmatic and you'd really best beware,

as for your closely held beliefs she doesn't give a care.

Debating her with a reasoned view, either now or later,

will only get you, sadly, called a racist homo hater.

So you tried to reason, you weren't a jerk.
That's when they all got you fired from work.
They claim to love justice, and equality too.
But if you disagree, they treat you like poo.

Cut me out!

Have you ever wanted to see things exactly like all your leftist friends see things? If so, simply snip out this cool pair of hipster glasses and tape over your eyes!

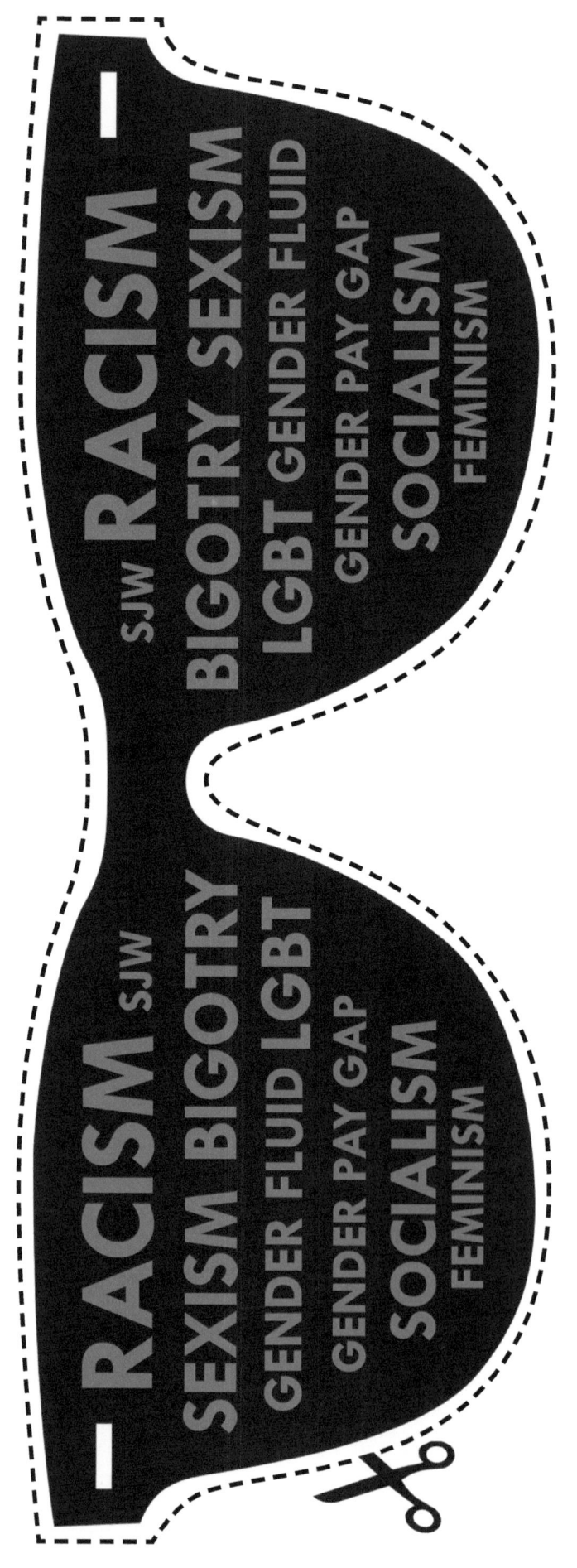

 *Cut out and proudly display!*

The Statist 10 Commandments

I. The State is your god. You shall have no others.

II. You shall pledge allegiance to your flag.

III. You shall not misuse the name of the State.

IV. Remember the Supreme Court and its holy decrees.

V. Honor thy politicians and workers of the State.

VI. Only your State may murder.

VII. You shall not love anything more than your State.

VIII. Taxation is NOT theft.

IX. You shall not expose your State's lies.

X. You shall not covet any rights apart from what the State gives you.

Color Me!

When I think about LEFTISM, I always get those warm and fuzzy COLLECTIVIST FEELS

Oh no!

Those evil capitalists are at it again! This time, they've created a complex maze of hard work for people to get lost in! Can you help us get through it to a glorious Welfare State?

The Maze of Sinister Free-Market Capitalism!

Socialist Utopia!

✶ Leftism 101 Word Search! ✶

```
I  B  F  D  E  F  E  M  I  N  I  S  T  K  L
A  L  G  B  T  Q  I  A  P  K  N  E  T  I  G
V  A  I  P  E  A  B  G  E  N  D  E  R  N  M
T  O  P  A  T  R  I  A  R  C  H  Y  T  S  T
O  H  B  Y  E  K  G  D  B  K  W  S  I  G  S
L  R  E  A  E  R  O  A  N  J  A  L  S  V  T
E  R  A  C  I  S  T  A  S  Y  A  S  T  I  A
R  E  G  A  L  I  T  A  R  I  A  N  L  D  T
A  C  C  E  P  T  A  N  C  E  E  S  Q  U  I
N  L  I  B  E  G  L  O  B  A  L  I  S  M  S
C  R  O  D  E  R  S  T  S  E  X  I  S  T  M
E  Q  U  A  L  I  T  Y  I  O  K  N  E  R  L
```

 *Yikes! An intolerant racist has tried to obscure certain words and names he feels uncomfortable with. Can you help find them?*

RACIST	SJW	GENDER
BIGOT	FEMINIST	LGBTQIAPK
SEXIST	TOLERANCE	GLOBALISM
PATRIARCHY	EQUALITY	STATISM
SOCIALISM	EGALITARIAN	ACCEPTANCE

Color Me!

Color Me!

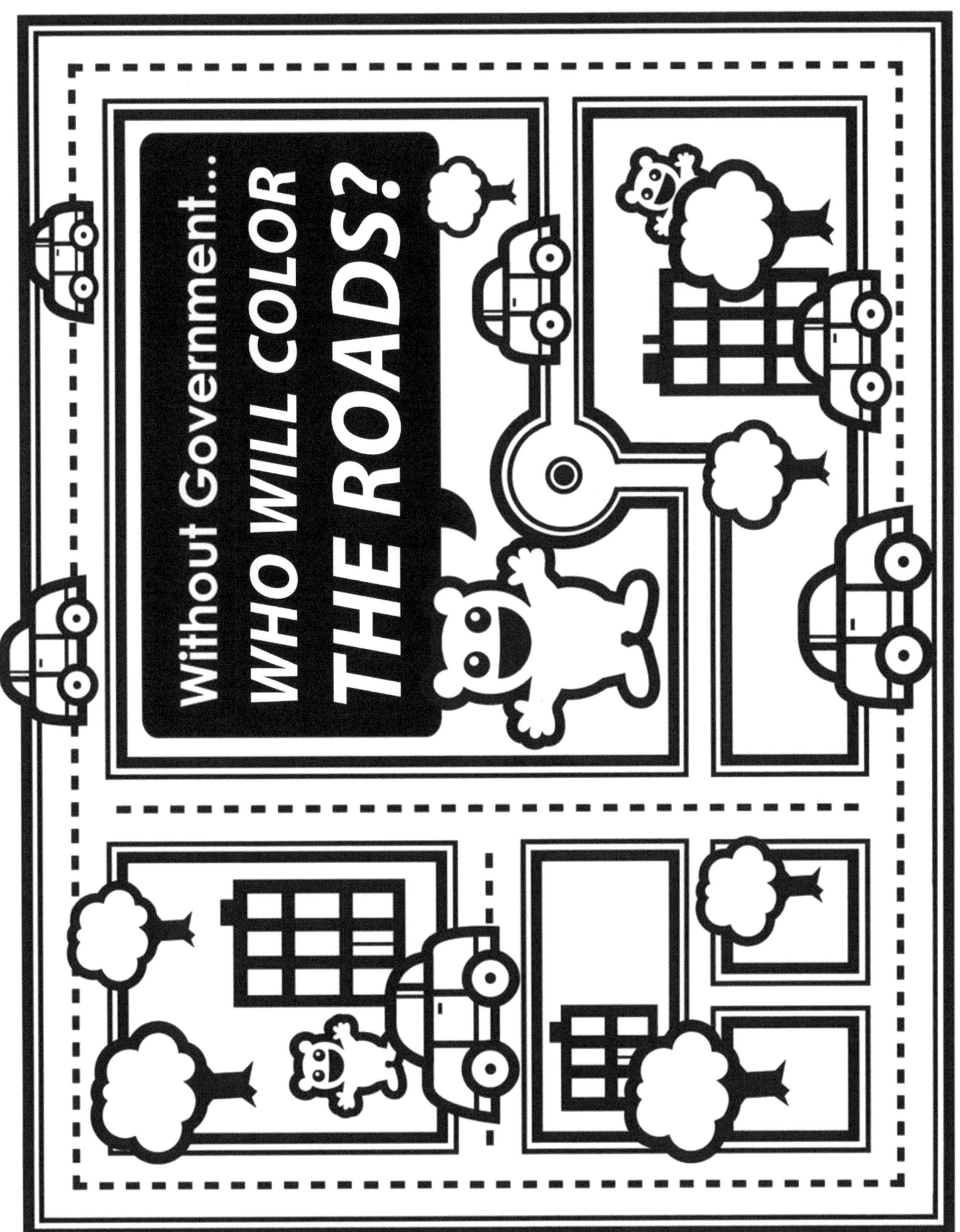

Color Me!

Captain Communist

Color Me!

> Oh don't look so glum... I'll only take around 30% of all you own, and then I'll be on my way!

Goldilocks the Socialist

Color Me!

What's this "mob rule socialism" thing I keep hearing about?

Capitalism	Socialism
We have to **work** for a living	I can sit on my butt and live off **welfare**.
People who have more than me **stink**.	State force ensures compliance and **peace**.
Rich people are **evil** and ruin everything.	Dissenters are sent to work camps.
Nothing is free.	Everything is "**free**".
Free markets will **destroy** the world	The State will **protect** the world...or else.
I wish we lived in a Star Trek utopia.	**Heaven** on Earth

Maybe we should #Try Socialism!

Mob Rule Socialists of America
www.mobrulesocialism.org

lookbook.com/mobrulesocialists
squawker.com/mobrulesocialists

Coming Soon to BSN

In 2061, a cyborg Lincoln kicks some intolerant conservative butt!

EVIL SOUTH

A BIASED AND HISTORICALLY INACCURATE PRODUCTION FROM THE CREATORS OF "SHAME OF CRONES"

Also don't miss...

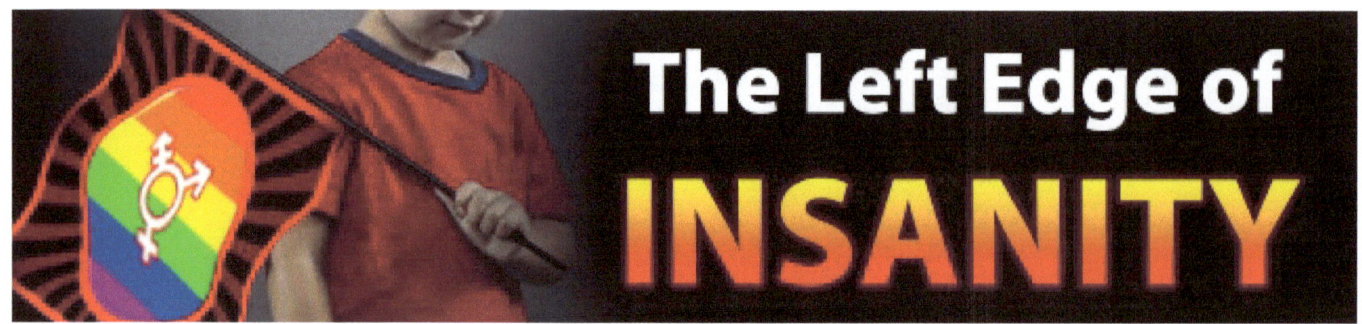

A Dystopian Short Story
As appeared on lewrockwell.com and abbevilleinstitute.org

To my fellow Associates: My name is Diversity-26, although my family and friends knew me as John before the Great Purge of Christianity. Today, as part of my punishment, I have been required to give you my story and beg you all for forgiveness for having disrupted your safe and happy lives.

According to the decrees of Democratic Socialism (or Dezism), I am a non-binary citizen of the Commune of Equality. The year is 142 E.T. (Era of Tolerance), and I live in the Quadrant of Purple, which is now referenced in history as The Great Wicked South Carolina by our State Educational Officers. Some of you may recall that I once wrote for <censored> before the Egalitarian Uprisings of 2020 P.T. (Pre-Tolerance), and the subsequent instituting of the Holy Doctrines of Leftism. In the years following, I was drafted into the Grand Army of the Antifa to fight the endless Wars of Southern Fascism – which many of our brave Associates continue to fight to this day. I served Rainbow Nation with honor, and was discharged seven years ago after losing my right arm and being blinded in my left eye by Fascist Free Market Shrapnel.

As tribute to my service, I was allowed to live within Progress City, a vast complex of prefabricated structures and shipping containers provided by our benevolent Dezi Party Officials. It was here that my Associates and I lovingly contributed to the advancement of Secular Multiculturalism and The Great All by encouraging positivity and harmony throughout the Quadrant of Purple. Some of the ways we shared in this happy task was through eliminating and censoring any images, artwork, books, movies, historical artifacts, music, etc. that may give offense to any group protected by the State. I am proud to say that we performed our tasks with remarkable efficiency, and 452,975 pieces of illegal material were incinerated under my watch alone.

But as stated by the Holy Doctrines of Leftism, it's only a matter of time before the sins of individualism, agrarianism, or capitalism burst forth and must be purged. My first offense was during the daily Weeping and Gnashing over the Crimes of the Past. The non-binary pre-pubescent life form the State provided me with happened to fall asleep during the ritual, and because I didn't want to be arrested for being a poor role model, I woke them up. However, my child felt their status as an Equal was threatened, and promptly contacted their Public School Watcher, who then notified the Hallowed Halls of the Southern Poverty Law Center. Thankfully, due to their dedicated inquisition, it was soon discovered that I had not only committed one, but two Equality Infractions. The second was for neglecting to let my dog sleep in my bed with me on a cold night. For both cases, I was placed on the SPLC's Map of Hate, and all Associates in the Commune of Equality were notified that I was a potential Child and Animal Abuse Predator.

My third offense occurred while communicating with friends on the Social Network known as Twitbook. I foolishly shared a photo of what I mistook for a beautiful statue that I discovered in a densely forested area beyond Progress City.

Progress City - Quadrant Purple

Although Twitbook algorithms ensured that only a limited few saw the image (unless I paid a special tax to boost the image to a wider audience), the Twitbook Internal Artificial Intelligence Network recognized the image as a potential violation and promptly notified the proper authorities. State Peace Enforcers quickly responded, and identified the picture as something called a Racist Remnant of the Putrid South. After deleting the image and offering grief counseling to those who had seen the offending image, they then put me on a weeklong suspension from the network. I don't know what the Confederacy was or how it was associated with this statue, but now, praise The State, I know it was a despicable thing. Furthermore, I have been assured the actual artwork will soon be destroyed secretly at night for the safety of all Associates throughout the Quadrant of Purple.

The High Priests of Tolerance had been merciful to me thus far, but the fourth offense I committed could not be ignored. I shudder to even mention it, but I was caught reading a book I should have liquidated. It was an ancient Book of Barbarism called *Uncle Remus*. I'm sorrowed to say that I was quite captivated by a picture in the front featuring an unusual white haired, dark skinned person talking to a rabbit. The stories within amused me, and made me think that perhaps those wretched people of the past might not have been as terrible as our schools, movies and books have lead us to believe. Of course, I now know this is false, as I was later reassured of the truth of Statism by being made to watch 72 hours of non-stop recordings from CNN, Fox News and Great Thinkers like Eric Foner and Bernie Sanders.

And so this brings me to the present. Fellow Associates, know that today I do not kneel in shame or embarrassment before you like a traitor, but that I stand proudly before you and our Rainbow Flag on global news feed. Like you, I have pledged allegiance to our State, and long ago signed my Oath of Loyalty in blood. I admitted to my sins against Rainbow Nation in Court, and was rightly sentenced by the Social Justice Tribunal for Political and Cultural Crimes against Life. As such, I will joyfully serve out 24 years of Equality Sensitivity Training at The Peaceful Way Re-education Gulag. This is likely the last time you will hear from me – for a while, at least, but hopefully not forever. Still, if it is, so be it. The State gives, and the State takes away. Blessed be the name of the State.

Perhaps somewhat shockingly, Lewis Liberman is a college grad, professional graphic artist, writer, award winning illustrator and totally awesome Gen Xer. He enjoys reading, being creative and spending time with family and friends. He also tries to follow the Lord, but sometimes falls flat on his face. Such is life.

Find out more at libertopiacartoon.wordpress.com.